real Samurai

illustrations by James Field
text by Stephen Turnbull

Over 20 true stories about the knights of old Japan!

ENCHANTED LION BOOKS
New York

To Joseph Turnbull, with best wishes from Grandad

First American Edition published in 2007 by
Enchanted Lion Books, 45 Main Street, Suite 519, Brooklyn, NY 11201

CONCEIVED AND PRODUCED BY Breslich & Foss Ltd., London
DESIGNED BY Balley Design Limited

Volume copyright © 2007 Breslich & Foss Ltd.
Illustrations by James Field
Text by Stephen Turnbull

Printed and bound in China

A CIP record is available from the Library of Congress

ISBN-10: 1-59270-060-8
ISBN-13: 978-1-59270-060-8

Contents

Introduction   4

The First Samurai

A flock of birds   6

Peasant soldiers   8

Challenges to combat   9

Warrior monks   10

SAMURAI FACTS: Archery   12
from horseback

The Great Civil Wars

The Battle of Ichinotani   14

Kamikaze!   16

A loyal samurai   17

A brave wife   18

The Battle of Dan no Ura   19

SAMURAI FACTS: The samurai   20
sword

Warlords of the Samurai

Splendid messengers   22

Becoming a samurai   24

27   Samurai and the arts

28   SAMURAI FACTS: Japanese armor

Guns and Christianity

31   East meets West

32   A woodcutter's son

33   Foot soldiers

35   The Battle of Nagashino

36   SAMURAI FACTS: Japanese castles

The Last Samurai Battles

38   Turtle ships!

40   Japan's new Shogun

41   The Shimabara Rebellion

42   The siege of Osaka castle

44   A strange character

45   Wandering swordsmen

46   SAMURAI FACTS: Bushido,
hara kiri, and the samurai

48   Glossary/Index

Introduction

T he samurai were the knights of old Japan. "Samurai" means literally "those who serve" and the first samurai were young men recruited to serve the Emperor of Japan. Their families became wealthy and known for their military prowess and some of them formed private armies and fought among themselves. In 1185 one samurai family, the Minamoto, took over the government of Japan and their leader became the Shogun (military dictator).

Proud Samurai

Samurai served their leaders with honor and were the only people in Japanese society allowed to wear two swords. A samurai was proud of himself and proud of his ancestors' military achievements. His greatest wish was to emulate them, and be remembered for his own brave deeds. A samurai was always well dressed and his jacket bore the family crest of the lord he served. The front of his head was shaved, and his hair was oiled and tied back in a neat pigtail.

The samurai had the right to kill anyone who disobeyed the law, but it was strictly forbidden for this right to be abused. Women rarely became samurai, but on page 18 you'll find out about one who did. However, women were trained to defend their lives if their homes were attacked.

A WELL-DRESSED SAMURAI

Samurai in battle

The Shoguns faced many rivals, and warfare was common for several centuries. On the battlefield samurai fought as part of an organized army. From the sixteenth century onward, the samurai's main combat weapon was the *yari* (a spear with a straight blade), which could be wielded from horseback or on foot. Some samurai were officers in command of other samurai. Yet others were in charge of large numbers of foot soldiers.

When on campaign, a samurai wore a suit of armor designed to provide maximum protection without restricting his freedom of movement, and his face was protected by a mask. Indeed, the masks often had grinning features and moustaches designed to frighten the enemy! A samurai's two swords were thrust through the belt outside his armor, on the front of which appeared his lord's crest.

THIS SAMURAI WEARS A SCARY MASK

A dying breed

In 1600, after many years of warfare, the Tokugawa family became Shoguns. Their rule was so strong that there were no major wars between rival families for over two hundred years. During that time the samurai still wore their two swords but had no one to fight. Instead, they became administrators and politicians, and when Japan joined the modern world in 1854 they found that their fighting skills were out of date. The age of the samurai was over.

A flock of birds

Minamoto Yoshiie was one of the most famous of the early samurai. During the eleventh century, he fought for the Emperor of Japan against rebels in the north of the country. He was a very successful leader, and his followers, many of whom were just rough foot soldiers, were inspired to fight for him with great bravery. Yoshiie had educated himself by reading classic Chinese books about warfare, and this learning saved his life. One day, he noticed birds rising in a panic from a wood, and remembered from his reading that this probably meant that his enemies had laid an ambush for him. His army surprised the enemy instead of the other way round! Yoshiie was well rewarded, and continued to serve the emperor with great loyalty.

Peasant soldiers

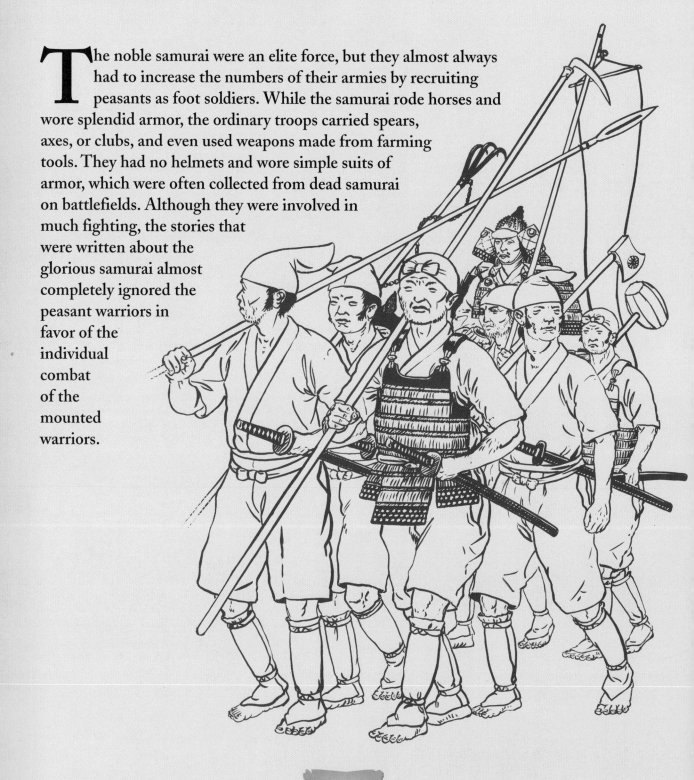

The noble samurai were an elite force, but they almost always had to increase the numbers of their armies by recruiting peasants as foot soldiers. While the samurai rode horses and wore splendid armor, the ordinary troops carried spears, axes, or clubs, and even used weapons made from farming tools. They had no helmets and wore simple suits of armor, which were often collected from dead samurai on battlefields. Although they were involved in much fighting, the stories that were written about the glorious samurai almost completely ignored the peasant warriors in favor of the individual combat of the mounted warriors.

Challenges to combat

On a typical samurai battlefield, hundreds of arrows flew and mobs of peasant warriors dragged samurai off their horses to kill them. But, whenever it was possible, a samurai preferred to engage in single combat with another enemy samurai. To do this he would shout out a challenge and hope that someone suitable would respond. If this happened, the two men would fight an archery duel from horseback. Sometimes, the men would carry on fighting on the ground with swords, daggers, or even bare hands. There was great honor to be had by defeating a famous opponent and, on rare occasions, there was even a pause in the battle while two famous champions fought each other. Traditionally, the loser would have his head chopped off by the winner!

Warrior monks

Samurai sometimes had to fight against armies of Buddhist monks recruited by powerful monasteries and temples that wanted to protect themselves. These monks were not gentle and kind like most monks, but were fierce fighters. In 1180, monks helped the Minamoto family against their rivals, the Taira, at the Battle of Uji. The battle was fought across the Uji River, which the monks and their samurai allies had defended by removing the planking from the bridge that crossed it. The Taira army arrived during a morning fog and some fell through the holes in the bridge! Many fierce hand-to-hand combats took place across the broken bridge, and monks and samurai fought each other with bows, swords, and *naginata* (curved spears). Three of the warrior monks—Godin, Tsutsui and Jomyo—fought so well that they became legendary for their bravery.

Archery from horseback

Although samurai are famous for fighting with swords, during the first centuries of their existence their skills with bows and arrows from horseback were more highly valued than swordplay.

Firing at the gallop

A samurai had to practice very hard to become a skilled horseback archer. He had to be able to control his horse while operating a bow and arrow, and this wasn't easy. In order to aim the bow and draw the string, the rider had to let go of the horse's reins and concentrate on his target. He could not do this for long, so his shots had to be fast and accurate. When practicing, the samurai would ride up and down a range and shoot arrows at small wooden targets. This skill has survived as the martial art of *yabusame* and is still performed at festivals in Japan today.

A SAMURAI DRESSED IN FULL HUNTING GEAR TURNS HIS BODY AND TAKES AIM WHILE HIS HORSE CONTINUES TO GALLOP ON AHEAD. HIS FEET ARE SECURELY PLACED ON THE HEAVY IRON STIRRUPS TO GIVE HIM THE STABILITY HE NEEDS TO HIT HIS TARGET.

Bows and arrows

The Japanese longbow was unique in the world because it was fired from one third of the way up its shaft. This meant that a samurai could control it better from a moving horse. The bow was made from long strips of bamboo cane glued together. To keep it secure its sections were wound around with rattan, a very flexible type of bamboo. The whole bow was painted with lacquer (a glue-like paint) to make it waterproof. The bow was very powerful and a man had to be strong to shoot it.

The arrows were made from sections of straight bamboo that were polished and lacquered. Different types of steel arrowheads were made. Some were for hunting; others were designed to pierce armor plates. One curious type was shaped like an open pair of scissors, which could cut through the cords that held an enemy's suit of armor together!

The arrows were carried in a "quiver" worn at the samurai's side. Quivers could take the form of little baskets or lacquered boxes, or might be covered in fur to keep the arrows dry. A samurai always carried a spare bowstring in case one broke in action.

TWO LONGBOWS (THE ONE ON THE LEFT IS IN A CARRYING STAND), TWO QUIVERS, AND A SPARE BOWSTRING REEL

A SELECTION OF DIFFERENT ARROWHEADS FOR THE SAMURAI LONGBOW

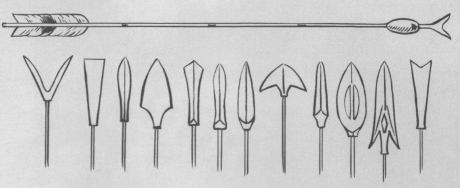

The Battle of Ichinotani

The Taira and Minamoto families fought a fierce series of campaigns called the Gempei Wars between 1160 and 1185. Minamoto Yoshitsune was one of the greatest heroes of the Gempei War. His victory at the Battle of Ichinotani in 1184 is famous for his surprise attack from the rear. His enemies from the Taira family had built a stockade fortress on the beach, but did not defend it from the rear because it was next to a steep cliff. While a diversionary attack went on against the fort early one morning, Yoshitsune, accompanied by the warrior monk Benkei, led his mounted army down a very steep mountain path. Some horses were hurt in the descent. The enemy's fortress was burned to the ground, but most of the Taira escaped to their boats, which were moored on the shore.

Kamikaze!

In 1274 and 1281 Japan was attacked by the Mongol armies of Khubilai Khan, the Mongol leader who had become Emperor of China. When the Mongols landed in 1274 they bombarded the samurai with exploding iron bombs, the first gunpowder weapons ever seen in Japan. The samurai fought back bravely against this surprise weapon, as well as against dense clouds of arrows, some of which were tipped with poison.

The Mongols withdrew, but returned seven years later with a much bigger army. This time fierce fighting by the samurai kept the invaders from landing, and raids by samurai in small boats forced them to stay on their ships. One night a fierce storm blew up and completely destroyed the Mongol ships. The Japanese believed this was an answer to their prayers and called the typhoon *kamikaze* – the wind from the gods.

A loyal samurai

From the time of the Gempei Wars, Japan had been ruled by a Shogun with the emperor relegated to a ceremonial position. In 1331, Emperor Go Daigo led an uprising against the Shogun's rule, and many samurai supported him. His most loyal follower was the hero Kusunoki Masashige, who held the Shogun's forces at bay from a series of mountain fortresses. Unfortunately, in 1336 Emperor Go Daigo ordered him to fight a pitched battle at Minatogawa against the Shogun's army. Masashige knew that he would lose, but he had to obey the commands of his emperor. Before Masashige left for the battle, his young son Masatsura promised to carry on his father's fight if he died. Masashige was indeed killed, and he is remembered today as the finest example of samurai loyalty. Masatsura fought on, and was killed in battle twelve years later.

A brave wife

Tomoe Gozen was one of a very small number of female samurai. She was the wife of Minamoto Yoshinaka, who fought against members of his own family. In the end, he was defeated by his cousin Minamoto Yoshitsune at the Battle of Awazu in 1184. When Yoshinaka knew the battle was lost he ordered Tomoe Gozen to leave him and save her life, but she had fought beside him for many years and was not willing to abandon him. Instead she led a valiant charge against the enemy and engaged one prominent samurai in single combat. After wounding him with the sharp curved blade of her *naginata*, Tomoe pulled him from his horse, held him against her saddle and cut off his head as a trophy. Only then did she obey Yoshinaka's order and flee to safety, leaving her husband to die on the field of battle.

The Battle of Dan no Ura

The Battle of Dan no Ura in 1185 was the final battle of the Gempei Wars. Unusually, it was fought at sea, but the two samurai armies of the Taira and the Minamoto began the battle by shooting arrows at each other almost as if they were on dry land. On one of the Taira ships was an important relative, the eight-year-old Emperor Antoku, whom the Minamoto desperately wanted to capture alive because that would make them the favored clan. When the Taira knew that the battle was lost, the emperor's grandmother took him in her arms and jumped into the sea, drowning them both. Nearly all the Taira samurai were killed, and it was said that the sea turned red with the blood of the dead and the dye from the Taira flags.

The samurai sword

The samurai sword is one of the most famous weapons in history. The finest swords were superbly crafted and a sword forged by a celebrated swordsmith was one of the most prized gifts a samurai could receive.

The swordsmith

The great swordsmiths treated their craft as a blend of science, art, and religion. They dressed themselves like priests before forging a particularly fine sword, which started life as only a crude lump of iron. This was beaten time and time again and heated in a furnace to make the finest steel. The raw steel was then folded and beaten repeatedly until the rough sword blade was like hundreds of thin individual blades welded together. A sword blade usually had a very hard cutting edge with a razor-sharp finish wrapped inside a body of springier steel that would prevent the sword from snapping. Finally, the sword was polished and mounted in richly ornamented fittings.

TWO ASSISTANTS HELP A SWORDSMITH BY BEATING THE PIECE OF IRON THAT WILL BECOME A SAMURAI SWORD

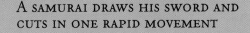

A SAMURAI DRAWS HIS SWORD AND CUTS IN ONE RAPID MOVEMENT

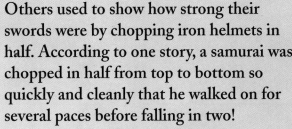

The sharpest weapon

The samurai did not use shields in battle because they could use their swords as shields. A skilled swordsman could deflect an oncoming blow and then respond with a killing stroke of his own. Hours of practice were given to the art of drawing the sword, because sometimes one cut delivered straight from the scabbard would be enough to win a fight.

One swordsmith boasted that his swords were so sharp that if a blade was placed uppermost in a stream and a water lily floated down toward it, the flower would be cut in two when it met the sword!

Others used to show how strong their swords were by chopping iron helmets in half. According to one story, a samurai was chopped in half from top to bottom so quickly and cleanly that he walked on for several paces before falling in two!

THE BLADE OF A SAMURAI SWORD, SHOWING THE HOLE FOR A PEG THAT WILL KEEP THE HANDLE IN PLACE

A FINE PAIR OF SWORDS, THE LONG KATANA AND THE SHORTER WAKIZASHI, MOUNTED FOR A SAMURAI'S USE AND PLACED ON A LACQUERED SWORD STAND

Splendid messengers

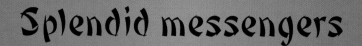

As the power of the Shoguns decreased, local warlords began to create their own territories, defended by samurai. The warlords who were leaders of samurai families were called *daimyo*, or "big names." As a battlefield could be a very confusing place, the *daimyo* used mounted messengers to keep up communications between different samurai units. The messengers were splendidly dressed so they could be recognized. All samurai wore little flags on their backs for identification, but the messengers had elaborate designs on their flags, or even sculptures made from papier-mâché or light wood.

Here one messenger wears a huge butterfly—the family crest of his *daimyo*. Another has a *horo*—a cloak wrapped around a light wooden frame that would inflate like a balloon when the samurai galloped. The third has a model of a Buddhist funeral tablet to show he is willing to die in battle. The fourth has a flag showing a demon taking a soul down to Hell. No one could fail to see these men in the heat of battle!

Warlords of the Samurai
(1392–1564)

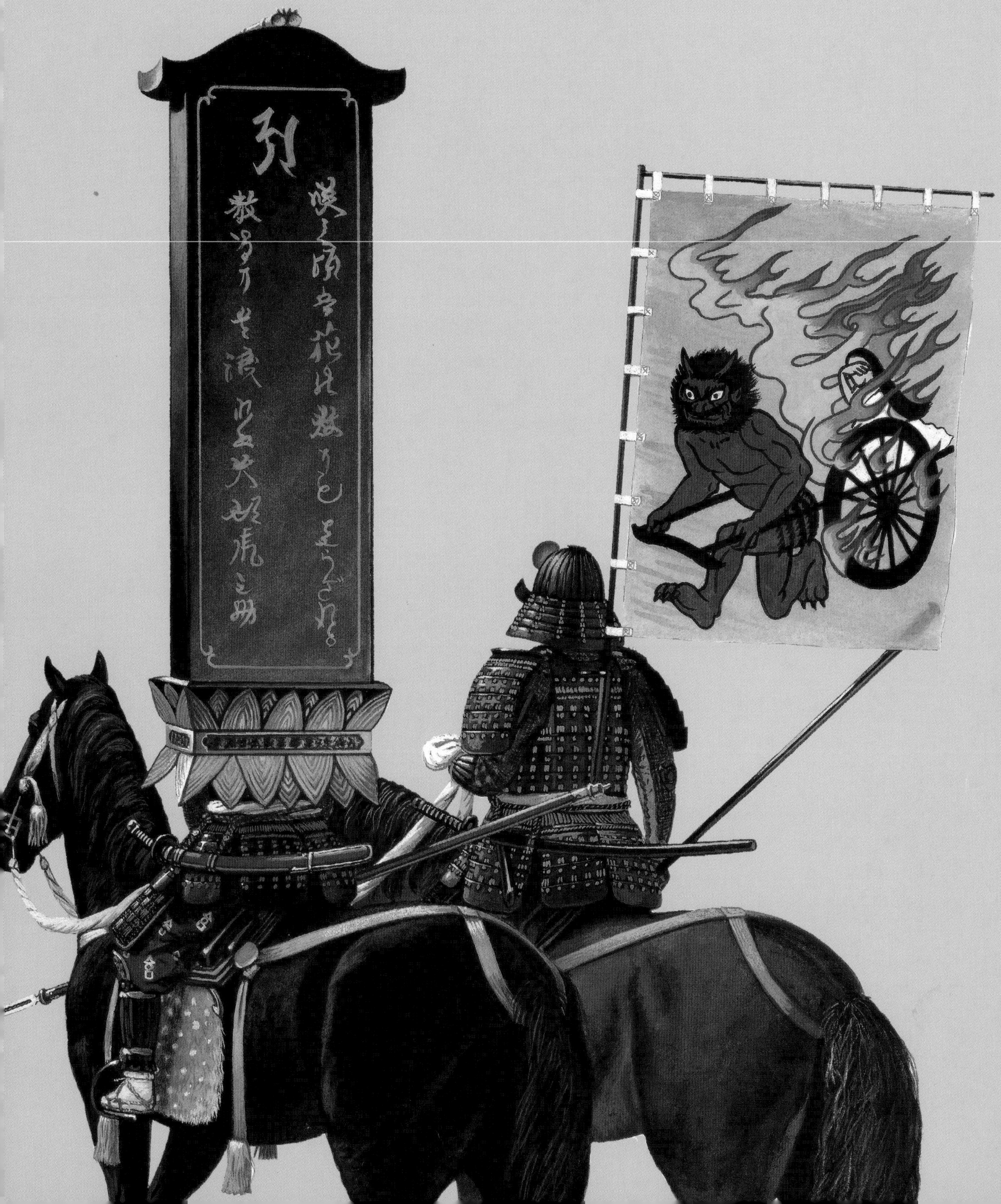

Becoming a samurai

A boy born into the samurai class was prepared from a very early age for the responsibilities that awaited him in adult life. His role as a warrior meant that he would be in training for his entire career. Archery, gunnery, horsemanship, wrestling, and spear fighting all had to be mastered, but pride of place was given to learning the techniques of sword fighting. As real swords were very sharp, even the most highly trained samurai could not use them for practice combat, so wooden swords were used instead. These were made of oak and were about the same weight as a metal sword. No protection was worn when practicing, so a young samurai could expect to receive many bruises!

A samurai was also expected to learn to read and write, which wasn't easy. The Japanese language used the Chinese alphabet and put words together from hundreds of different characters, all of which had to be memorized. Hours of practice were given to writing the characters using a brush and ink. Paper, which was made from mulberry leaves, was expensive, so sheets of paper were used time and again for practice. Eventually the surface of the paper was completely black, and the teacher could only see how well the boy had written the character by the wetness of the ink the student had used.

A very important moment for a young samurai was when his father took him into battle for the first time. He would probably be kept at the rear for his own safety, but in 1536 Takeda Shingen saved his father's life during his first battle at the age of fifteen! A few years later, this young man banished his father and become a powerful *daimyo*.

Real Samurai

Samurai and the arts

As well as being brave and fearless warriors, samurai were also meant to enjoy things like poetry and painting. A love of the arts was as important as military skills if a samurai warrior wanted to be a good leader in peacetime. His home might have views of an exquisite garden or the gardener might use tricks to give the impression of a distant landscape. Small trees and large rocks would be arranged neatly, sometimes with a pool or a stream. Inside the house a samurai might enjoy being entertained by a wandering blind *biwa* (lute) player, whose songs and poems were often about the heroic samurai of the past. The samurai would sip tea as he sat on the smooth *tatami* (straw mats) enjoying a moment of peace.

Japanese armor

The suits of armor worn by samurai were very different from those worn by European knights, who went to battle in chain mail or suits made of large steel plates. Japanese armor makers used small iron or leather scales that were lacquered to protect them against rust and then laced together with rawhide to make horizontal strips. A number of these strips was then combined using strong silk cords to make different armor plate sections that would fold naturally around the samurai's body.

Yoroi

The earliest samurai armor made from these plates was called *yoroi* and was like a big square box. It had large shoulder plates that acted as a shield and a sheet of patterned leather across the front to make a smooth surface for the bowstring when the samurai was shooting arrows. The helmet was a heavy iron bowl with a wide neck guard of armor plating.

Crested helmets

When guns were introduced during the sixteenth century, stronger armor was needed, so heavier steel sections were made. These were lacquered and combined

TWO ARMOR MAKERS USE STRONG SILK CORDS TO LACE TOGETHER BODY ARMOR AND A HELMET

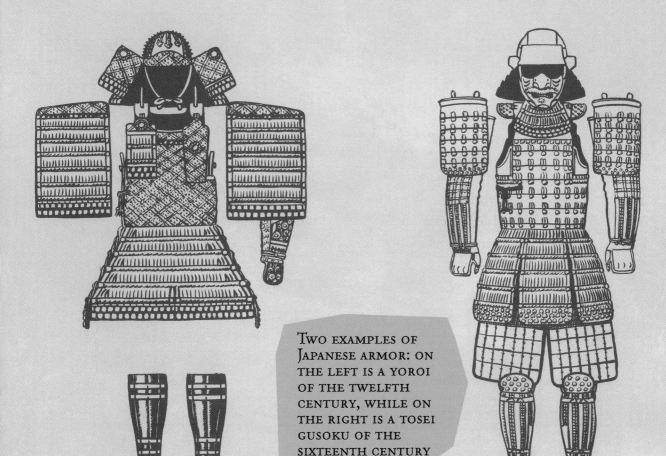

TWO EXAMPLES OF
JAPANESE ARMOR: ON
THE LEFT IS A YOROI
OF THE TWELFTH
CENTURY, WHILE ON
THE RIGHT IS A TOSEI
GUSOKU OF THE
SIXTEENTH CENTURY

to produce a suit of armor that could be
bullet proof. At the same time, protection
for the face was introduced in the form of a
mask. These later styles of armor were very
plain, so many samurai made them look
more splendid by wearing fantastically
shaped helmets. Some helmets had
decorations such as feathers, golden crests,
or enormous buffalo horns.

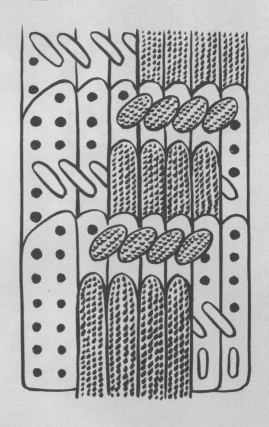

THIS DETAIL OF A SECTION OF ARMOR
PLATE SHOWS HOW INDIVIDUAL SCALES
WERE LACED TOGETHER AND THEN
COMBINED WITH OTHER ROWS TO MAKE
A COMPLETE ARMOR PLATE

East meets West

In 1543 a group of Portuguese merchants was shipwrecked off the coast of Japan. The unexpected appearance of the strange foreigners was a big surprise, but what really interested the samurai were the muskets that the men carried. These arquebuses (guns fired by dropping a burning match onto the touch hole) were the first European firearms seen in Japan and, although the weapons were quite primitive, the samurai realized how useful they would be in war. Visits by merchants were encouraged, and Christian missionaries soon followed them. The great *daimyo* Oda Nobunaga (page 35) allowed the priests to preach freely in his lands because he then received special favors from the merchants. As the years went by, both Christianity and the use of firearms spread widely throughout Japan.

A woodcutter's son

The great leader Oda Nobunaga was skilled in using firearms but he also had an eye for talent. He recruited into his army a brave peasant soldier called Toyotomi Hideyoshi, who rose rapidly through the ranks and proved to be one of the best samurai in history.

In 1582, when Hideyoshi was off campaigning, a traitor surprised Oda Nobunaga while he was asleep and had him killed. Hideyoshi immediately marched his army back and defeated the traitor. This victory impressed everyone and gave him the opportunity to inherit all of Nobunaga's territories. More battles followed and after a few years Toyotomi Hideyoshi managed to defeat all of his other rivals. All the other *daimyo* submitted to him and the civil wars ended in 1591. Japan was united once again, this time under a man who was the son of a humble woodcutter.

Foot soldiers

Ordinary foot soldiers fought next to samurai warriors for centuries, but they only became valued by military commanders in the sixteenth century when firearms and larger armies came into use, which meant they had to be better organized and more disciplined. Oda Nobunaga began the process by dressing his foot soldiers in simple suits of armor that became their military uniform. Toyotomi Hideyoshi

(opposite) continued the trend, and his armies included large squads of spearmen, archers, and gunners who wore their leaders' badges on the front of their armor. They fought in large, well-organized squads alongside the sword-wielding samurai. From being casually recruited peasant soldiers who often deserted, the new-style *ashigaru* (foot soldiers) had become professional warriors who now made up the lower ranks of the samurai class.

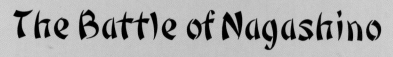

The Battle of Nagashino

In 1575 the *daimyo* Oda Nobunaga had a chance to test his idea that European firearms could change Japanese warfare for ever. One of his castles, called Nagashino, was being besieged by Takeda Katsuyori. Oda Nobunaga knew that the greatest strength of the Takeda samurai was their use of rapid charges on horseback. As he drew near to the castle, Nobunaga erected a loose fence and stationed thousands of his foot soldiers behind it, armed with arquebuses. For the first time, the proud samurai were kept to the rear, but the gamble paid off. When the Takeda samurai charged, the gunners, under the strict discipline of samurai like Honda Tadakatsu (seen here with his deer-antler helmet), broke their impact with volleys of bullets. Nobunaga's samurai then advanced and won the battle. After Nagashino, other *daimyo* copied Oda Nobunaga's idea of how to use firearms.

Japanese castles

At the center of each *daimyo*'s territory was his magnificent castle. It acted as his military headquarters, providing storage for weapons and food, and barracks for his army. The earliest castles made use of the plentiful supplies of wood available from Japan's forests, and looked a little like the stockade forts of the American West.

The yamashiro

The castle builders also made clever use of the numerous hills and mountains in Japan. A *daimyo*'s *yamashiro* (mountain castle) would be strung out along adjacent peaks, connected by wooden walls. In time, builders began clearing hillsides to create open spaces where towers and gateways could be erected. To reinforce the surrounding ground, castle builders clad the mountainside in stone, producing the massive stone bases characteristic of Japanese castles. These stone bases were so strong that some have even survived bombardment by modern weapons.

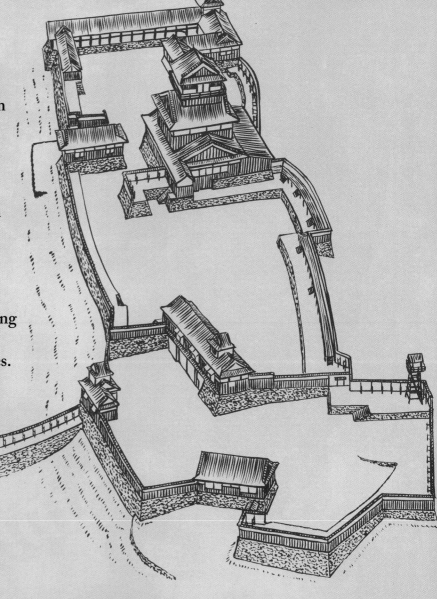

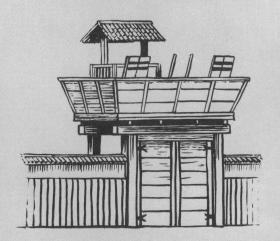

Gateways

The approach to a castle was deliberately made difficult for an attacker who would have to make several twists and turns through walls and gateways before he came anywhere near the keep. He could be watched at every turn and fired on from above. Long plastered walls with loopholes for bows and guns ran along the edges of the massive stone bases. Castles built on flat land were defended by a series of dry ditches and wet moats as well.

The castle keep

If the foundations were strong enough, very large buildings, such as multistory castle keeps, could be built on top. Some keeps were very beautiful. They had graceful curved tile roofs and were coated in clay to make them fireproof. They were usually painted white and could be seen from a long distance away.

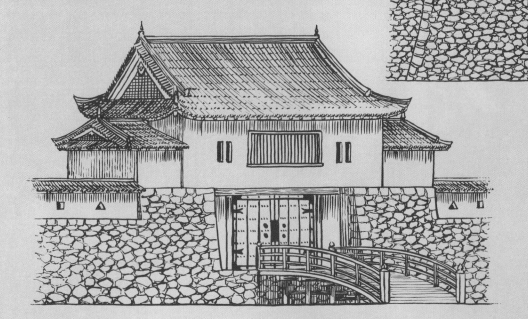

Turtle ships!

After Toyotomi Hideyoshi had beaten all the *daimyos* in Japan (page 32) , he began to get big ideas about conquering China. However, to invade China his armies would have to pass through Korea. When the Korean king refused to help, Hideyoshi ordered his armies to invade Korea in 1592. The Korean army was quickly defeated, but their very strong navy under the command of Admiral Yi Sun-sin began to attack the Japanese transport ships with turtle ships. These strong wooden battleships were shaped like turtles and armed with cannon, one of which was fired through a dragon's head in the bow! Admiral Yi Sun-sin soon destroyed many of the clumsy Japanese ships. Because the Japanese could not get supplies to samurai fighting on land, they began to lose battles there, too. In 1598 the samurai were driven out of Korea by the Chinese army, and Hideyoshi's plans ended in failure.

Japan's new Shogun

Wearing a suit of armor made from a Spanish model presented by European traders, Tokugawa Ieyasu (page 42) defeated the rest of his rivals at the Battle of Sekigahara in 1600. The battle was fought through rain and fog in a narrow valley and Ieyasu only clinched his victory when one of the enemy *daimyo* changed sides. After the battle, Tokugawa Ieyasu revived the ancient title of Shogun and became Japan's new military dictator. His capital, a little fishing village called Edo, grew to become the great city of Tokyo, where Ieyasu's descendants ruled for the next 250 years. These years are called the Tokugawa Period. It was a time of peace, but of peace enforced by the strict rule of the Tokugawa family.

The Shimabara Rebellion

Apart from the siege of Osaka castle (page 42), the only serious challenge mounted against the Tokugawa family was the savage Shimabara Rebellion of 1638. Most of the rebels were Christians. The Tokugawa government was very suspicious because it was afraid that Japanese Christians would encourage an invasion from Spain. Christianity was therefore banned and its followers were cruelly persecuted. Sustained by their faith, the Shimabara rebels held out for over a year against the Tokugawa samurai, but they were all killed when their castle fell. To prevent further rebellions, the government closed Japan off from further contact with Europe. This isolation of Japan lasted until 1854 when American ships arrived and Japan was forced to open its doors once again. When faced with modern weapons the samurai realized that their days were over.

LOW AD · SEIA OSACTISSIMO · SACRAMENTO ·

The siege of Osaka castle

Toyotomi Hideyoshi died while his armies were still in Korea (page 38). His son, Toyotomi Hideyori, was then only five years old and it looked as though Japan was going to dissolve into chaos again because the country had no leader.

A fierce civil war began, but was soon won by a *daimyo* called Tokugawa Ieyasu who took over power from young Hideyori, while allowing him to live. This was a mistake because when Hideyori grew up he led a rebellion against the Tokugawa family. In 1614, he packed tens of thousands of *ronin* (unemployed samurai), many   of whom had lost lords and lands to the Tokugawa, into the huge castle of Osaka. When Tokugawa Ieyasu realized that Osaka castle could not be captured, he bombarded it with huge cannon brought from England and Holland. A peace treaty was agreed, but Tokugawa Ieyasu cheated. Despite protests from Hideyori, his men filled in the outer moats and in 1615 the Tokugawa army returned and captured the weakened castle. Hideyori died in the flames as Osaka was burned to the ground.

A strange character

Miyamoto Musashi was one of the greatest samurai swordsmen who ever lived, but he was a very strange character. He always looked very untidy and hardly ever washed. His specialty was to fight with a sword in each hand, but he was also known to defeat rival swordsmen using sticks or branches, or, in one case, the oar from a boat.

However, his control of a real samurai sword was so good that it was said he could balance a grain of rice on a man's forehead and cut it in two without breaking the man's skin! Miyamoto Musashi fought many duels, but was also renowned for his skills at painting. Several of his pictures, painted using only black ink, have survived to this day.

Wandering swordsmen

Swordsmen like Miyamoto Musashi (opposite) traveled around Japan challenging rivals to contests so they could display their skills. These contests became popular during the period of peace under the Tokugawa family and large crowds would gather to watch the action. Real swords were rarely used. Instead, a duel with wooden swords was enough to show which of the two samurai was champion. Occasionally, an arrogant samurai would try and attack a wandering swordsman with a real sword and end up being killed himself. Many of the wandering swordsmen were offered large sums of money to stay with a particular *daimyo* and teach sword fighting to his samurai. These *sensei* (teachers) started schools of sword fighting that became famous throughout Japan. They were the founders of *budo* (martial arts), which eventually took the place of samurai skills.

Bushido, hara kiri, and the samurai

The unwritten code of conduct of the samurai was called *bushido*: the "Way of the Warrior." A samurai had to serve his lord in life and death, and if his lord or his father were murdered, *bushido* demanded that revenge should be taken. One celebrated tale is of two daughters called Miyagino and Shinobu, whose father was murdered by a samurai. Realizing that they did not have the skills to avenge him, they studied the martial arts in secret for many years. Eventually their moment came and one of the girls caught the samurai's sword in a *kusari-gama*, a weapon made from a sickle with a long weighted chain attached, and her sister finished him off with a *naginata*! This long spear with a curved blade was the traditional weapon used by women when they needed to protect their homes.

SISTERS MIYAGINO AND SHINOBU WAITED FOR THEIR VICTIM AND KILLED HIM WITH A NAGINATA AND A COMBINED SICKLE AND CHAIN WEAPON

A BUDDHIST PRIEST KNEELS AND PRAYS AT THE GRAVE OF A SAMURAI KILLED IN BATTLE

Samurai religion

The samurai followed two religions. One was Shinto, an ancient faith that worships thousands of *kami* (Japanese gods) who lived in mountains, rivers and waterfalls. The Emperor of Japan was believed to be descended from the *kami* of the sun. The other religion was Buddhism, introduced from China. By the time of the samurai, the two religions had mingled. Shinto was concerned with birth and life. Buddhism concentrated on death, and Buddhist priests would go to battlefields to pray for the souls of dead samurai.

Honorable deaths

It was considered a disgrace to be killed by an anonymous bullet or arrow. Instead, samurai preferred to fight a worthy opponent, face-to-face. When the loser was dead, the winner would cut off his head as a trophy and present it to his commander to prove he had done his duty.

If a samurai was defeated or knew he was going to die, the honorable thing to do was to commit *hara kiri* by cutting open his stomach. *Hara kiri* was so painful that a friend was allowed to help by cutting off the samurai's head.

Glossary

arquebus a musket fired by dropping a lighted match onto the touch hole

ashigaru a disciplined foot soldier who fought beside the samurai

biwa a musical instrument like a lute

budō the martial arts learned by samurai

bushidō the "Way of the Warrior," the samurai code

Daimyō a Japanese warlord who ruled his own small territory

hara kiri an honorable act of suicide by cutting open the belly

horo a stiffened cloak

kami the gods of the Shintō religion

kami kaze the typhoon that sank the Mongol fleet in 1281

katana the longer of the two samurai swords

naginata a spear with a long curved blade

rōnin a samurai without a master to serve

samurai a member of the military class of Japan

sensei a teacher of swordsmanship or martial arts

Shōgun the military dictator of Japan

tatami straw mats in a Japanese house

tosei gusoku later styles of Japanese armor, often of plain design

wakizashi the shorter of the two samurai swords

yamashiro a castle built on a mountain

yari a samurai spear

yoroi early armor, often very elaborately decorated

Index

A
Admiral Yi 38
archery 9, 12, 24
armor 5, 28–29
arrows 9, 12–13, 16, 28
art 27
ashigaru 33

B
Benkei 14
bow 13, 28, 37
Buddhism 8, 10, 21, 47
bushido 46

C
castles 36
challenges 9, 45
Christianity 31, 41

D
daimyo 22, 25, 31, 32, 35, 36, 37, 40, 42, 45
Dan no Ura 19

E
education 24-25
emperor 4, 6, 17, 19, 47
Europe 31

F
face mask 5, 29
firearms (see guns)

G
gardens 27
Gempei Wars 14, 17, 19
guns 28, 31, 32, 33, 35, 37

H
hara kiri 47
Honda Tadakatsu 35
horo 22

I
Ichinotani 14

K
kami kaze 16
katana 21
Khubilai Khan 16
Korea 38
Kusunoki Masashige 17
Kusunoki Masatsura 17

M
messengers 22
Minamoto family 4, 10, 14, 17, 19
Minamoto Yoshiie 6

Minamoto Yoshinaka 18
Minamoto Yoshitsune 14, 18
Miyamoto Musashi 44, 45
Mongol invasions 16

N
Nagashino 35
naginata 10, 18, 46

O
Oda Nobunaga 31, 32, 33, 35
Osaka 42

P
peasants 8, 9, 33
poetry 27

R
religion 47
revenge 46
ronin 42

S
Sekigahara 40
Shimabara Rebellion 41
Shogun 4, 5, 17, 22, 40
sword 4, 5, 20, 21, 46
sword practice 24, 44, 45

T
Taira family 10, 14, 19
Takeda Katsuyori 35
Takeda Shingen 25
Tokugawa family 5, 41, 45
Tokugawa Ieyasu 40, 42
Tomoe Gozen 18
Toyotomi Hideyori 42
Toyotomi Hideyoshi 32, 33, 42
turtle ships 38

U
Uji 10

W
wakizashi 21
warrior monks 10
women 4, 18, 46

Y
yabusame 12
yari 5